TLINGIT TALES

Potlatch and Totem Pole

LORLE K. HARRIS

Illustrated by Dorothy Mandel

To my son, Frank Werner Harris, and to the memory of Robert Zuboff who shared the wish to preserve these Tlingit legends.

Library of Congress Cataloging in Publication Data:
Main entry under title:
Tlingit Tales, Potlatch and Totem Pole.

Legends as told by Robert Zuboff, head of the Beaver Clan at Angoon, Admiralty Island.
1. Tlingit Indians—Legends.   2. Indians of North America—Alaska—Legends. I. Harris, Lorle. II. Zuboff, Robert.
E99.T6P68   1985   398.2'08997   85-8853

ISBN 0-87961-153-7

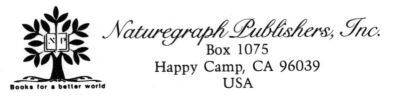
Naturegraph Publishers, Inc.
Box 1075
Happy Camp, CA 96039
USA

Books for a better world

CONTENTS

The prow of a Tlingit canoe at sea (also on cover).

THE TLINGIT & THEIR LEGENDS

Good stories are everywhere, stored in the memories of family and friends, adding sparkle to family reunions, or helping pass the hours in a hospital. It was at the Indian Health Service Hospital in Mt. Edgecumbe, Alaska, that my son, Frank, a student intern, recorded legends of the Tlingit People as told by a patient, Robert Zuboff. Head of the Beaver Clan at Angoon, Admiralty Island, the eighty-year-old chief was one of the few remaining Tlingit who still spoke his native language. After he retired from his trade as a fisherman, he spent many hours in Angoon classrooms sharing tribal lore with the children to assure the survival of the Tlingit traditions.

Robert Zuboff's stories picture the atmosphere of a little known Indian culture far more vividly than a textbook description of customs and beliefs. Although there are differences among the Northwest Pacific Coast tribes, the similarities in their legends and customs suggest they descended from the same ancestors.

The tribes were divided into two phratries, which in turn were subdivided into subclans, each having its own crest. Inheritance was usually through the maternal line. The Indians raised totem poles in memory of their dead, to keep a record of their ancestors, and to list the legends of the tribe. The business of the tribe was carried on at the potlatch feast.

The early missionaries did not understand the use of or importance of the totem pole and potlatch. They thought of the totem poles as "graven images" and destroyed them. In their eyes the potlatch feast was a heathen orgy in which the natives foolishly squandered their possessions instead of saving them for a time of need. The missionaries could not have been more wrong.

Among people without a written language, the potlatch was a court where the leaders were publicly given the privileges and duties of tribal offices. The elders used the occasion to pass on to the younger people the history and traditions of the tribe. Men told of brave deeds, exciting adventures and supernatural events. Their stories added to their prestige and that of the clan. The tales would be repeated at the next potlatch, and the next, and become part of the tradition of the tribe.

Elaborate rules provided for the orderly conduct of both business and social activities. The gift-giving of which the missionaries disapproved was actually like putting money in the bank. Those that received gifts promised to give even more valuable presents in return at a later date; they returned the gifts with interest.

The chief invited the guests, but the entire clan took part in the potlatch. The more potlatches the chief gave, the more gifts he passed out, the more important he became. To strive constantly for higher rank was a way of life for these people, and competition was keen. Once he won high rank, a man had to work to keep it.

Sometimes a man inherited high rank. Then it was up to him to prove he deserved it. The totem pole beside his house told of the accomplishments of his ancestors, a reminder for him to daily "go forth and do likewise."

As with all stories passed along by word of mouth, the legends exist in several versions. Sometimes parts of a story are woven into an entirely different tale. A collection of legends tells a great deal about a people's outlook on life.

The Tlingit legends show the Indians' respect for nature and their sense of being a part of nature. Not only do the Indians trace their ancestry back to an animal, but the heroes of their legends slip in and out of animal form with great ease. The Indian kills for food, but thanks his victim for providing him with something to eat. He gives human characteristics to his animal ancestors. He speaks of animals as "land otter people" or "fish people," imagining them living in villages much like his own.

The Tlingit give human characteristics to natural events, too. Robert Zuboff describes the thunderbird as "a fierce person in the air . . . When he breaks the mountain down, the sparks fly and you hear the thunder . . . He spins the earth . . . Even Columbus didn't know the earth was spinning, but the Indians did!"

The Indians had a strong belief in the supernatural. They also believed that certain people had greater powers than others. These became shamen, or medicine men. They thought otters or wolves or other creatures sometimes captured men. When they returned to their tribes they were able to prophecy future events and cure illnesses.

Many of the legends describe how well-known medicine men secured their power. Others explain natural occurrences, landmarks and place names. Each clan has a story telling how it got its crest. And parents have a string of stories to teach proper behavior.

Come share with me some legends of the Tlingit.

"Swinging a huge club in his hand, the giant bore down on the boy like a boulder cut loose by a rockslide."

STILL SAVAGES

Long, long ago, so long ago that no one even remembers their names, three Tlingit brothers lived in the rugged mountains near Lake Atlin. Their food supply was running low, so the oldest brother set out alone to hunt. Hours passed and he didn't come back.

The second brother went into the woods to search for his brother. Hours passed and he didn't return either.

Something dreadful must have happened, the youngest thought, as he set out to search for his brothers. As he went deeper and deeper into the woods it grew darker and darker. The hooting of the great horned owl sent shivers down his back. The seventeen-year-old was afraid, but he clenched his teeth and pressed on.

A shaft of light filtered through the cleft ahead where the trail led between two mountains. Suddenly a shadow blocked the opening. It was a savage! Never had he seen such an enormous man! The boy's muscles stiffened like icicles. He couldn't move.

Swinging a huge club in his hand, the giant bore down on the boy like a boulder cut loose by a rockslide. Closer and closer he came. He raised the club over the boy's head and brought it down with the force of a stone adze splitting a cedar.

The boy awoke with a terrible headache. He could hardly move or breathe. In the dark his body doubled over and swayed gently in regular rhythm.

The boy stretched. He stubbed his feet against a taut barrier. He remembered the club coming down over his head, but nothing else. Where was he? Gradually he figured out what was happening. The savage had put him in his packsack and was carrying him home for dinner. He reached for his cutting stone, then stopped. No, he would wait for a better chance to escape.

At last the giant stopped. He lifted the bag off his shoulders and laid it on the ground. The boy listened until the sound of his captor's footsteps disappeared. He has gone into his house, he thought; now's my chance! He twisted and wriggled in the sack until he was able to reach his cutting stone. He hacked a big slit in the sack and got out.

The boy stretched and looked about. The savage's club leaned against the wall of the house. Now it's my turn, the boy thought. He picked up the club, tiptoed over to the doorway and waited.

Before long the giant came out. With all his strength the boy brought the club down on the big man's head, knocking him to the ground! The boy clubbed the savage again, and again, and again.

The boy stared at the prostrate body. I know I killed him, he thought, but he killed both my brothers. What more can I do to hurt him?

The boy gathered brush and dry leaves into a huge pile. He dragged the lifeless form to the pile and placed it on top. The boy knelt beside the heap, and rubbed two sticks together until a spark was kindled, then another, and still another. The sparks fell on the dry leaves and burst into flame, which burned long and brightly until there was nothing left but a heap of snow-white ashes.

The boy stared at the ashes. I know the savage is finished, he thought, but he killed both my brothers! What more can I do to hurt him?

Impulsively he took a deep breath and blew on the ashes. They danced and twirled as they rose into the sky.

Suddenly the hum of countless mosquitoes filled the air and descended in a cloud on the boy. And that is why to this day mosquitoes are out for blood. They are still savages!

SAKI, THE BOY HUNTER

Famine threatened the village that was the home of Saki, the boy hunter. Every day the men went out in search of food. Some climbed into their canoes armed with spears, nets and fish hooks. Others slung quivers filled with arrows over their shoulders, and clasping their bows firmly in their hands, trudged into the woods. Every day they came home with a few little fish and a skinny rabbit or two – only a mouthful for each villager after the food was divided.

Saki, too, went out every day. Although he was known for his skill with the bow and arrow, his luck wasn't any better than the men's.

One day when Saki hunted, he came upon a little animal that looked like a dog, but he was so bedraggled and dirty, Saki couldn't be sure. He took the dog home and washed him. He shared his meal of porcupine meat with his new friend, giving him the larger portion. Then to be sure he wouldn't mistake the dog for his prey when hunting, he dabbed red paint on the animal's head and feet.

The very next day, Saki and the dog went into the forest. The dog flushed out grouse from their hiding places and brought them to Saki. He tracked down a mountain sheep. Saki was so pleased with his hunting companion, he gave him the best part of the meat. The remainder Saki shared with his family and friends.

When Saki's brother-in-law saw what a fine hunting dog Saki had, he asked to borrow the animal. Saki put red paint on the dog's feet and around his mouth. "You may take him," Saki said, "but be sure to give him the first sheep you kill. That is what I always do."

When the man returned from the hunt, the dog was not with him.

"The flickering flames from the hearth cast eery shadows on the cave-like walls of the underground house. Saki strained his eyes to make out the stooped figure of a tiny woman."

"Where is my little dog?" Saki asked.

"He ran away."

That's strange, thought Saki, he must have had a reason for running away.

Saki went to his sister. "What did your husband do with my dog?" he asked. "Tell me the truth."

"He threw entrails to the dog," she said. "The dog refused to eat them and ran straight up between the mountains."

"I was afraid that would happen."

Saki went to his brother-in-law. "Show me where the dog disappeared."

His brother-in-law took Saki to the spot where the dog fled into the mountains. Scrutinizing every inch of ground for footprints smudged with red paint, Saki plodded along. At last he found them.

The footprints led to a large lake. Saki saw a town on the far side, but how was he to get across? He paced back and forth. If only I had a canoe, he thought.

After a while the smell of smoke tickled his nose. His eyes watered. Was that a column of smoke curling up from beneath his feet? Saki stepped to one side.

A door in the earth opened and a woman's voice said, "Come in."

Saki felt his way down the log ladder with its wedge-shaped footholds. The flickering flames from the hearth cast eery shadows on the cave-like walls of the underground house. Saki strained his eyes to make out the stooped figure of a tiny woman.

"What brought you here, Grandchild?" she asked.

Saki told her of the dog he befriended, and how the dog had helped him, but was now lost.

"Your dog must be the Wolf Chief's Son," the old woman said, "he lives on the other side of the lake."

"But how . . ."

The old woman read his mind. "Take my little canoe. Don't worry, it won't turn over with you. When you have carried it to the shore, shake it and it will become large enough for you. But don't paddle the boat," she continued, "lie down in the bottom. Concentrate on where you want to go and the canoe will take you there."

Saki did as he was told and landed safely on the other side of the lake. When he stepped out of the boat, he wished the canoe small. He watched the canoe shrink smaller and smaller. It shrank so much, Saki folded it and put it away.

Saki walked along the beach until he met some boys playing with a deeply arched bow. Its colors flashed blue, red, yellow and green as they tossed the bow about.

"Where does the Wolf Chief live?" Saki asked.

The boys pointed to a house at the far end of the village.

Saki slipped into the house. He crept behind the wolf people gathered around the hearth – and there, lying in front of his father, was Saki's friend.

"I feel the eyes of a human being upon us," the Wolf Chief said. "Where is he hiding?"

The little wolf put his nose to the ground and followed the man-scent to Saki. Little wolf was so happy to see his friend, he jumped up on him and licked his face.

Then the father knew who the boy was. "I am pleased that you cared enough to search for my son. I sent him to live among your people because I knew you were starving and he could help you. We are happy to have you as our guest."

Little Wolf and Saki played by the fire. The wolf people brought Saki bear and mountain sheep meat to eat.

When the time came for Saki to go home, the Wolf Chief said, "Some of your people didn't treat my son properly. He will not return to the village with you, but I will give you some charms instead."

He had hardly finished speaking when Saki saw the Wolf Chief had taken the form of a human being. The man pointed to a fish-hawk's quill hanging on the wall. "Bring it to me," he ordered his son.

The Wolf Chief took the quill in his hand. Squinting his eyes, he aimed the quill at the opening above the hearth. The quill flew through the smoke hole. Wolf Chief motioned to Little Wolf to get the quill.

"Whenever you meet a bear, Saki, point the quill directly at him," Wolf Chief said, "and it will pierce his heart." He handed Saki the quill.

Then Wolf Chief showed Saki a large robe, neatly folded and tied like a blanket. "This is the mantle of life and death," he said gravely. He unfolded the robe. "This side cures illness. Place the soft warm fur next to the sick person's skin – so."

He shook the mantle so it billowed like a blanket buffeted by the wind, then settled gently on the ground. He turned the mantle over. "The hide side is rough and cold. It will bring death." Handing Saki the mantle, he said, "Use it wisely."

Saki turned to leave.

"Do you see that great curved bow the boys are playing with?" Wolf Chief asked. "That's my rainbow. When you see it in the evening sky, it warns of bad weather. Take shelter 'til the sun comes out. If you see it in the morning, it will be a fine day."

Then the chief put a pebble-like object in Saki's mouth. It tasted sweet as blackberries and succulent as the tenderest of meats. "Take this," the Wolf Chief said, "Although the days of your journey will be many, they will seem but a few."

And so it was. When Saki came to the cleft in the mountains where Wolf Chief's son had disappeared, he knew he was almost home. He hurried along the path that led to his village.

Suddenly a huge grizzley stepped out of the woods, rearing up in front of Saki! Saki drew the magic quill from his pocket, and aimed it straight at the bear. Just as Wolf Chief had said, the quill flew directly toward the bear's heart!

Shortly afterward, Saki came upon a flock of mountain sheep. The sheep were grazing so close together it was impossible to single out one animal. Saki aimed his quill at the flock. One by one the sheep toppled over!

Saki examined his prey. The quill struck every one of the sheep, he thought wonderingly. He cut up the meat. When he came to the last sheep, he found the quill embedded in its heart.

Saki ate a little, then dug a cache in the ground. My people will have enough meat to last a long time, he thought. He covered and marked the cache so he could find it again.

Now Saki could hardly wait to get home. He ran so fast his feet barely touched the ground.

The village was strangely quiet when he reached the row of houses facing the sea. No children played on the beach. No murmur of women's voices, chatting as they went about their work, reached his ears. Where was everyone?

Saki ran toward his house. His little cousin lay in front of the doorway. Saki bent over her. She looks like a bundle of bones, he thought, placing his ear against her chest. There was no heartbeat!

Saki quickly unwrapped the mantle the wolf chief had given him. He threw it over the little girl, making sure the life-giving side touched her body.

The child stirred. She stretched out her arms as if awakening from a night's sleep. "Saki, Saki," she said, "where have you been?"

"Visiting the wolf people. Where's everybody?"

"They're all asleep."

Saki crept inside the house. Silence enveloped him like a thick blanket of fog. He climbed on the sleeping platform where his aunt and uncle lay. Both were dead. Saki threw the magic mantle over his uncle, and then over his aunt. They sat up!

"I've plenty of food for everyone," Saki said proudly. "I'll wake up everyone and we'll go after it." He pushed aside the blankets that separated his family's sleeping quarters from the next. He visited each section of the sleeping platform in turn, waking each person with his wonderful robe.

Then Saki led his people to the place where he had stored the meat of the mountain sheep. What a feast they had! What they couldn't finish, they carried home.

After that, whenever the people needed meat, Saki hunted with his magic fish-hawk's quill. When his people fell ill, he cured them with his magic blanket. And the people paid him for his services, so that he became a very rich man.

Blankets and furs, finely carved feast bowls, and painted storage boxes piled up in his house. When he had enough gifts for the chiefs in the neighboring villages, he held a great potlatch and gave away all he had.

Again and again Saki invited his neighbors to a giveaway feast. After each potlatch his wife took his cedar root hat and added a new strip to the topknot to commemorate the event. From the height of his hat everyone knew Saki was a great and powerful man.

"After a while he saw the giant grizzley with the white-tipped fur step out of the woods. Behind him trudged another bear, and another, and another."

POTLATCH FOR BEARS

Son-of-a-Glacier was the only living person left in the great house that was the home of the Iceberg Clan. One by one his relatives had sickened and died, wiped out by a plague that had killed so many in his village.

Son-of-a-Glacier piled driftwood in the large central hearth in the great house. He lighted the fire and watched the shadows play against the empty tier of sleeping rooms that circled the building. The silence was unbearable.

Even a lonely man has to eat, so he put a piece of halibut on a stick and roasted it over the fire. He dipped the fish into some eulachon grease and put it in his mouth. He had no appetite for food. He looked sadly at the pebbles bordering the hearth, sparkling white and pink in the reflection of the flames; but he had no eye for beauty. Life has to be shared to be enjoyed.

But how? He couldn't paddle away in search of new friends. People would think a man alone had been chased out of his village for practicing witchcraft or flaunting the taboos of his tribe. He might just as well be dead.

Son-of-a-Glacier doused the fire and trudged off into the woods. He came upon a bear trail. Ah, he thought, I'll let the bears kill me; I'll lie down across the path and wait.

By and by he heard the crunch of bushes breaking under the weight of heavy feet. He looked in the direction of the sound. Sure enough, there were several grizzlies plodding along behind a giant fellow with white-tipped fur.

Cold shivers rippled over Son-of-a-Glacier's back. He didn't want the grizzlies to tear him apart. He jumped to his feet, stretched to his full height and waited. When the leader of the bears came near, Son-of-a-Glacier said, "I've come to invite you to a feast."

The huge bear's fur bristled along his back. "Man is the killer of bears."

This is the end for me, thought Son-of-a-Glacier, but he put on a brave front. "I've come to invite you to a potlatch," he repeated, "but kill me if you wish. I don't mind. I'm all alone. My wife, my children, my friends, are all dead."

The grizzley turned around. He whined to the other bears. They all turned around and disappeared into the woods.

Son-of-a-Glacier sighed with relief and hurried back to the village.

"What's the rush?" asked one of the villagers.

"I go to prepare a feast," he said. "I've invited the grizzlies to be my guests."

"Whatever made you do such a foolish thing?" asked the man. "Didn't the plague kill off enough of us? Do you want the entire village to be wiped out?" Without waiting for an answer he ran away.

He'll warn the others to lock themselves up in their houses, thought Son-of-a-Glacier.

When Son-of-a-Glacier returned to his house he removed the sooty stones from the hearth and replaced them with bright white pebbles. A potlatch called for a clean house.

Because it was a special occasion he took off his shirt and decorated his body with scarlet stripes; one over his heart, one across the upper part of his chest, and more on his upper arms.

Rising early the next morning, he took out the huge feast bowls carved of cedar logs, and filled them with berries, the fat of the eulachon fish, and three kinds of smoked salmon. Then he went outside, and stood beside the doorway to wait for his guests.

After a while he saw the giant grizzley with the white-tipped fur step out of the woods. Behind him trudged another bear, and another, and another.

The few villagers who were about hurried into their houses.

Son-of-a-Glacier ran to greet his guests, escorting them to his home. He seated the big grizzley in the place of honor at the center of the rear of the house. The others took their places around the walls on either side of their leader. As Son-of-a-Glacier seated each bear he called out the name of the dead man whose place he was filling.

Each bear, in turn, said, "Thank you."

Then Son-of-a-Glacier brought out the trays of cranberries and salmon and eulachon fat. The bears ate and ate and ate.

When they were finished, the giant grizzley stood up on his hind legs. He raised his right foreleg, pointing to the smoke hole above the hearth.

Gesturing with his left foreleg, like a tribal leader waving his arms as he spoke at a potlatch, he said, "The grizzlies thank Son-of-a-Glacier for a feast worthy of the Iceberg Clan. May the Clan multiply and rise again in greatness to equal the generosity of our host."

The big bear lumbered over to the doorway. "Lie down, Son-of-a-Glacier," he said.

Son-of-a-Glacier lay down. The grizzley bent over the man and licked the red stripes on his arms and breast.

"I am licking away your sorrow," he said.

Then he turned to the other bears. "Be a friend to this man. Each one of you show him your respect."

One by one the bears approached Son-of-a-Glacier and licked him. Then they left as they had come, in a single file behind their leader, the grizzley with the white-tipped fir.

And Son-of-a-Glacier was never lonely again because he had learned the way to win a friend is to be one.

" 'Whoo . . . . Whoo . . . . Whoo . . . .,' she hooted.
She flapped her wings and flew away."

HOW THE OWL CAME TO BE

A young woman lived with her husband and mother-in-law in the town of Sitka. She enjoyed walking along the beach and watching the waves break over Herring Rock, a huge, flat boulder at the water's edge.

During the herring season the tide swept over the rock, carrying countless fish with it. When the tide receded, the herring slipped back into the sea.

What a waste, the young woman thought; I will have to do something about that. She trudged along the shore until she came to a path that led into the woods. Tall hemlocks grew on both sides of the trail, their slender branches touching the ground. How like a seine was the network of needle-fringed twigs that formed the dense foliage!

The woman tore branches from the hemlock and stripped bark from a cedar tree that grew nearby. Twisting the strands of bark into string, she bound the branches together to make an apron. With the apron around her waist, she walked to the beach and waited for the tide to rise.

At last the waves broke over Herring Rock. The young woman waded into the water. "Come on, fish," she said. "I am your wife."

Just as she had planned, the herring caught their fins and tails on the prickly branches, flapping this way and that. If a fish freed himself from one cluster of pine needles, he caught his fins on another. Before long, the young woman's apron shimmered with the bodies of tens of silvery fish.

The young woman untied her apron and shook it, spilling the fish on the beach. The herring wriggled in the sand, trying to reach the water, but she quickly gathered them up in her basket.

When the basket was full, the young woman hid her apron in the woods and hurried home with her catch. What a meal she would have! And she wasn't going to share it with her mother-in-law either!

She waited until the old woman was out of the house before roasting the fish over the open hearth fire. But the aroma of the roasting fish brought her mother-in-law running.

"My, that smells good," she said, "What are you eating?"

The young woman quickly gulped down the last bite. "Nothing," she said.

The next day, when her husband was out seal hunting, she cooked another herring.

Again her mother-in-law came running. "You must be eating something," she said. "May I have a taste?"

The young woman speared the entrails of the herring with her roasting stick and held it in the fire. When the entrails were red-hot, she dropped them into her mother-in-law's hand.

"Ow," shrieked the old lady as the fiery entrails seared her skin. "My son shall hear about this!"

Her daughter-in-law only shrugged. For once she was going to eat all the herring she wanted. Wasn't she the one who made the clever fishing apron?

After a while her husband came home. His mother was waiting for him. The young woman watched her mother-in-law take her son aside. They huddled together, whispering.

When her husband left without speaking to her, the young woman went out after more fish, but she forgot her basket.

"Bring my basket," she called, shaking the herring out of her hemlock apron. "Bring me my basket!"

No one answered her call. Her voice grew hoarse as apron after apron-full of fish squirmed on the beach. "Bring me my basket!"

Darkness fell. Still no one answered her call. The young woman could no longer form words. "Whoo . . . Whoo . . . Whoo . . . " she hooted. She flapped her wings and flew away.

Even today, when a young girl is selfish, her parents admonish her, saying, "Don't put fish guts in your mother-in-law's hand, or you will become an owl."

And the mountain that rises from the beach at the place where the young woman disappeared is still called Mount Owl.

"He followed the people along the stream and into the waters of Carter Bay. Just then, for the first time in days, the rays of the sun burst through the cloud cover on the western horizon."

THE BOY WITH THE COPPER NECKLACE

It had been a long, cold winter at Kasaan on Carter Bay in southeastern Alaska. The Arctic air seeped into the sheltered inland passage, raising great banks of fog that shut out everything more than a man's length away. The fog muffled the shrieks of the wind that blew in from the Pacific Ocean to the southeast. The Tlingit fishermen pulled their boats out of reach of the battering sea and waited out the storm in their clan houses.

Great hunks of smoked salmon and halibut, as well as deer and bear meat, once hung in the smoke houses. But now the winter food supply was nearly gone and the fog and rain kept the fishermen at home. A furry green mold grew over the last of the fish. The people scraped the mold from the fish and ate it.

But not Auktatsi. "Ick," he said, making a face. "I can't eat that."

"Eat and be thankful," said his mother, "or the fish people will get you."

"Fish people!" the boy scoffed. "They can't get me. Besides, I'm not hungry." He played with the copper chain that hung around his neck.

After a while he went out. He walked along the Carter River where it flows into the bay. The weather had grown warmer. A heavy fog lay like a great curtain over everything. Auktatsi threw rocks into the stream and listened for the "plop" they made as they hit the water.

He played with the stones for a long time, until he heard the buzz of many voices above the rushing stream. The voices grew louder as shadowy shapes emerged through the fog. A large crowd of people surrounded Auktatsi. They seemed to float above and beside the river.

"Where are you going?" Auktatsi asked.

"On a far journey to a beautiful place," said an old man. His long gray hair fell over his shoulders blending with the soft gray robe that shimmered when he walked like the silver scales of a salmon. "Would you like to come along?"

Why not, thought the boy. He followed the people along the stream and into the waters of Carter Bay. Just then, for the first time in days, the rays of the sun burst through the cloud cover on the western horizon. They spread a golden glow across the sky that flowed over the water like a lighted pathway. The shining light hypnotized the boy and he walked deeper into the water. Not until the sun dipped below the mountains did he realize that he was swimming in a school of fish and that he was one of them.

There was nothing to do but follow. For days and days the fish swam. Finally they came to the city of the fish people. It was in a mammoth cave, so huge the boy didn't know where it began, or where it ended. He saw only the icicles hanging from above, lighting the city with a soft silvery radiance like that of the moon. All about him were dwellings of the fish people, all kinds of fish people: sockeye people, dog salmon people, halibut and herring people.

All the people were dancing and singing and eating. For three long years the fish people went to one potlatch after the other.

At last the fish grew tired of partying. They swarmed out of the city, Auktatsi swimming with them. Day after day they pressed on until they came to Cape Chacon. There the fish separated into two schools. One turned toward Cordova Bay, the other toward Carter Bay.

Auktatsi joined the fish swimming to Carter Bay. When he reached Kasaan, his old home, he swam close to shore. There on the beach he saw a woman cleaning fish. He swam closer for a better look, leaping into the air with joy as he recognised his mother. She was too busy to notice him.

"Eye-ow!" he called as he jumped again. "Eye-ow!"

His mother looked up. "Eye-ow!" she cried.

Auktatsi swam to the very edge of the water. Again he jumped into the air.

Fast as an eagle swooping down on its prey, his mother darted into the water and caught him in her bare hands.

Auktatsi squirmed as she picked up her knife. He wriggled this way and that, trying to get away. Her clasp was too strong. Her knife came down on his neck. Ping!

The knife hit something hard. His mother groped under the scales with her fingers. There, around the neck of the fish, was a copper chain.

"This is no ordinary fish," she said out loud. She dropped her knife, picked the fish up in her arms, and hurried to the medicine man.

"Look at this fish," she said. "He wears a copper necklace like Auktatsi."

"That fish is your lost son," the shaman said.

"A son in fish scales? Whatever shall I do with him?"

"Put the fish on top of the smoke house and let the rain fall on him for three days."

So the woman placed the fish on the roof of the smoke house. And for three days the rains came. The raindrops pelted the fish with the force of hailstones. Auktatsi felt his scales loosening. Finally the drops fell in a gentle shower and washed the scales away.

Auktatsi slid off the roof. It was good to feel the firm ground under his feet. He touched his copper chain. The necklace and the shaman had saved his life. He, too, would become a medicine man and help his people.

Auktatsi became a powerful medicine man. He became famous for his ability to prophesy future events. Even before the clouds gathered on the horizon, or the winds began to blow, he knew a storm was brewing. He warned his people to pull their canoes out of the water and seek shelter.

Before he died, Auktatsi called his people together. "Give me back to the sea from which I came," he said, "and I will pound my drum to warn you when a storm is coming."

You can still hear his drum today. When a southeaster blows out of the Pacific, wind-whipped breakers crash into a huge cave on the shore of Carter Bay. The cave echoes with the boom, boom, boom of the surf and the people know their prophet speaks.

KAHASI, THE COWARD

In the days before the Tlingit had weapons, there lived a young man named Kahasi. He was the nephew and heir of the great chief, Galwet. Kahasi was kind and gentle, but he had one failing. He was a coward – at least that's what the young hunters called him.

Kahasi knew he angered these young men because he slept warm and snug in his blanket while they plunged into the icy sea after Galwet. That was no way for a chief's heir to behave. He should bathe and wrestle with the others to build strength for the sea lion hunt, but Kahasi went his own way.

When the young men returned from their icy dip, drenched and shivering, they commanded Kahasi to bring logs for the fire.

They order me about as though they were the heirs of Galwet, and I a mere slave, Kahasi thought. But it was easier to obey than to argue, so Kahasi fetched the firewood. He even clowned a bit, groaning under the weight of the logs as if it required great effort to drag them to the hearth.

"Weakling!" scoffed a hunter.

"You call yourself Galwet's heir," said another.

Kahasi paid no attention. He walked over to the far side of the fire where the boys, not yet old enough to hunt sea lions, wrestled.

"Come, wrestle with us," a young cousin called.

Kahasi rolled on the ground with the boy and when he thought the boy had had enough, Kahasi let the child throw him.

"Shame on you, Kahasi!" a young man called out. "You let a child beat you!"

Kahasi ignored his tormentor. He was only pretending

"The man-killing sea lion glared at Kahasi from the top of a huge flat rock."

weakness, while he waited for the right moment to prove himself a worthy heir of Galwet.

At night, when all were asleep, Kahasi slipped out of the house. He built a fire on the beach to light the darkness. Then he ran and splashed in the shallow water until he was so exhausted he had to float to rest his feet.

When he came out of the sea, Kahasi threw water on the fire. He placed his blanket of finely woven cedar bark on the ashes and lay down. Billowing puffs of steam enveloped him in a great cloud, soft and warm as down. He dreamed of the day when he would bring home the biggest sea lion of all. What smacking of lips there would be as the people feasted on their favorite meat. How great would be his standing in the village!

Gradually the cloud drifted away and the mat grew cold. Kahasi picked up the blanket, threw it around his shoulders, and crept back into the house.

One night as Kahasi bathed, he heard the cry of a loon above the soft lapping of the waves. Following the sound, he met a short, heavy-set man dressed in a bearskin.

"Come, wrestle with me," said the man. He grasped Kahasi's upper arms.

His clasp is like the grip of a wolf's jaws, Kahasi thought, as the man forced him to the ground. Kahasi tugged to the right. He tugged to the left. He kept a firm grip on his opponent, but couldn't budge him.

At last the man jerked loose. He stood up. "You're not strong enough yet," he said, "but you will be. I'll work with you until you're as strong as a grizzley."

"Who are you?" Kahasi asked.

"I am Latsin (Strength)," said the man. "Keep our meetings secret and you shall share my power."

After that, when he bathed at night, Kahasi listened for the whistle of the loon. And when he heard it, he followed the sound. Night after night he wrestled with Latsin.

One night Kahasi pinned Latsin to the ground.

"Now," said Latsin, "you are strong. Don't go into the water again." He pointed to a sturdy cedar. "Go to that tree and pull out the lower limb."

Kahasi went, and with one tug he pulled the branch from the tree.

"Now replace the limb."

Kahasi did. The limb looked exactly as it had before.

"Now go to the next tree. Twist it down to the roots."

Kahasi did as he was told.

"Now untwist it again."

Kahasi did. The tree looked exactly as it had before.

Kahasi hurried home. He had hardly settled in his sleeping place when the young men rose for their morning bath. One of them climbed up to the sleeping platform and pulled Kahasi's hair to awaken him.

Kahasi snored, but he was only pretending. He was far too excited and happy to sleep. At last he was ready to test his strength against the others. No more would they call him the weak one.

Kahasi listened to the shouts of the men as they bathed in the icy water and wrestled with each other on the beach. Suddenly a great hurrah, like the blending of a multitude of cheering voices, echoed through the early morning. A few minutes later, a second burst of applause broke the stillness. Whatever could that be about, Kahasi wondered drowsily, and dropped off to sleep.

He was awakened by one of the chief's wives. She shook him roughly. "Your uncle has torn a limb from the great cedar – you could never do that!"

And the chief's second wife said, "You, Galwet's heir! You sleep like a chief, while he bathes like a hunter. This morning he twisted a tree right down to the roots. You'll never inherit your birthright!"

So that was what the noise was about, Kahasi thought. He smiled to himself. The time had come for the sea lion hunt.

All that day Kahasi watched the townspeople go out to see the trees that bowed to the mighty muscle of their chief. He watched the young men readying the canoe for the hunt.

"Kahasi will sit in the bow," one fellow teased, "so he can land first and tear the biggest sea lion in two."

The others laughed and went on with their work.

That night Kahasi bathed secretly.

The next morning he went to the older of the chief's wives. His aunt occasionally slipped him something to eat because she felt sorry for him. "I need a clean shirt and food," he said.

"Who asked you to go on the hunt?"

"No one, but I'm going anyway."

So his aunt gave him a clean skin shirt and a package of smoked fish.

Kahasi ran down to the boat.

"Don't let him come. Don't let him come," the young men called. They plunged their oars into the water and pushed off.

Kahasi waded after them. He grasped the stern of the canoe. The young men pounded his fingers with the oars to force him to let go. Kahasi pulled the boat back on the beach and climbed aboard.

"You couldn't kill a rabbit," a hunter scoffed.

"Leave him alone," Chief Galwet ordered. "He can bail out the boat for us."

But the hunters went right on taunting Kahasi – all the way to the rocky island where the sea lions lived.

"Kahasi's going to tear twenty sea lions in two!"

"Kahasi has the strength of a grizzley!"

"Don't get your feet wet when you leap ashore, Kahasi!"

Kahasi said nothing.

It was almost impossible to beach a canoe on the treacherous wet rocks that formed seal island. Galwet waited until a big wave swept the canoe skyward on its crest, then jumped to the island.

Kahasi watched his uncle pick up a small sea lion and dash it against the rocks. Next Galwet tackled a huge fellow that had been edging close to him. Galwet jumped astride his tail, threw his arms around the lion's neck and wrestled with it. The gigantic sea lion gave a tremendous lurch, throwing the hunter against the rocks. Galwet tumbled into the sea in an avalanche of boulders. He disappeared in a mighty splash that nearly capsized the canoe.

Wails of anguish broke from the hunters' throats. The paddlers backed away from the island.

"Galwet must be avenged," Kahasi called out.

Expressions of surprise and shame flickered across the men's faces.

Kahasi put on his skin shirt and his hair ornament. "I pulled the limb out of a tree," he said. "I twisted the cedar down to its roots. And I will kill the sea lion."

He moved toward the bow, shoving the men aside with the ease with which a man pushes aside small branches blocking his path in the woods. "Take the canoe closer to the island," he ordered.

The men cringed, but obeyed.

When the canoe rose again to the crest of a wave, Kahasi lept ashore. Two small sea lions yapped menacingly. They rushed toward him. With a blow of the fist he killed first one and then the other. He walked over them, with as much unconcern as if they had been tiny mice.

The man-killing sea lion glared at Kahasi from the top of a huge flat rock. Kahasi glared back as he walked slowly and steadily toward the animal. Suddenly Kahasi pounced on the sea lion and tore him in two. He picked up the sea lions and carried them on his back to the water's edge.

The men maneuvered the canoe ashore. They gasped in surprise to see Kahasi carrying all three sea lions at once. They marveled at the size of the animal that had killed their chief.

"You shall be our chief," said a man who had mocked Kahasi earlier. "We know now you are worthy to be heir of the great Galwet."

And Kahasi became famous for his great strength – so famous that his feats were imitated at feasts to encourage other young men to follow his example.

"We found you adrift on a log with countless birds flying above you and around you."

THE MAGIC SINEWS

A long time ago there lived near Sitka a middle-aged man named Kaka. Kaka's pretty wife was many years younger than he. Sometimes he thought she paid entirely too much attention to the young men of the village, but he pretended not to notice. He brought her meat and beautiful furs so she would have no cause for complaint.

One day Kaka brought home an especially handsome land otter. His wife skinned the animal and put the hide out to cure. Then she took the sinews from the tail and twisted them with green yarn to make ear ornaments. When she had finished she went to her husband.

"Come here, dear," she said, dangling the ornaments in front of him. "Look what I made for you. Let's take off those old things you're wearing and put on these new ones."

She removed the old ornaments and threaded the sinews through the holes pierced along the rims of his ears.

Not long afterward, Kaka and his wife went to a nearby island to gather yellow cedar bark for the new community house. All day long he worked in the woods stripping bark from the trees while his wife gathered berries. When evening came, she came to get him.

"I'll need help to get the cedar bark down to the canoe," Kaka said.

"I won't do it. I won't do it!" his wife said, running away.

Angered by her disobedience, Kaka picked up a stick and hurried after her. She slid down the path like a child on an icy hill, disappearing suddenly in the underbrush. Then Kaka knew that the creature was not his wife, but a land otter woman.

A few weeks later, Kaka and his wife returned again to

the island. He had forgotten all about the incident.

Toward evening his wife came to get him. "Kaka, come," she said, "or our fish stew will spoil."

"I'm coming." Kaka hurried after the woman, following her all the way to town. Suddenly he stopped stock-still. The people walked about dragging otter tails behind them! Once again he had been tricked by the land otter woman. He had followed her to her home.

Kaka looked this way and that for a way to escape, but there was none. I'll bide my time, he thought. After a while he noticed the people looked human again. Their otter tails had disappeared.

"We're going to the next town," the woman said. "Won't you come along?"

Kaka nodded grimly. He knew he had no choice.

The land otter people took Kaka to Prince of Wales Island. On the beach they met a beautiful young girl walking with her father. Her black hair gleamed like the polished horn of a mountain goat. Her eyes sparkled like spray dancing on sunlit waves.

Several of the men stopped to talk to her father. Suddenly they pushed Kaka toward the girl's father. He grasped Kaka's upper arms firmly from behind. Kaka couldn't move.

The land otter men took the young woman by the hand and led her away. They had exchanged Kaka for the girl. Kaka was now a slave.

"Your work is to bring in the halibut," his new master ordered.

One day when he brought in a load of fish, Kaka saw an old woman cutting up halibut on the beach. She looked very familiar to him. He walked toward her and the old woman looked up.

She stared steadily at Kaka for a few minutes.

"You're Kaka," she said. "Do you remember your aunt who was lost when her canoe turned over? I am she. I was captured by the land otter people."

"When I was a little boy, yes, I remember."

"Now the land otters have captured you. It was your wife's fault. She tied those land otter sinews in your ears. Here, let me take them out."

Kaka sat down on the sand while his aunt gently removed the ornaments from his ears.

"My husbands are building a canoe. When it is finished, we will take you back to Sitka where you belong."

True to her word, when the boat was completed, Kaka's aunt came after him. Her husband, Bucking-the-Tide, sat in the bow and her husband, Tail-End-Going-Down-Into-The -Water, sat in the stern.

"Lie down in the bottom of the canoe," Kaka's aunt ordered. She covered him with a cedar bark blanket and sat down beside him. "When we come to the place we are going, sit astride the first log you see," she said.

Kaka lay in the bottom of the canoe a long time – so long, he could feel kelp growing on his back. Would they never reach their destination?

At last Kaka heard his aunt say, "Hurry, hurry, it's getting light."

Kaka knew that the early morning hour of death was at hand – when the cry of the raven flies through the air like a poison arrow to strike down any animal that may be about.

"Sing, Bucking-the-Tide," the old woman urged.

Bucking-the-Tide sang in a voice deep as the rumble of distant thunder:

"Oh, Current-Running-Toward-The-Shore
Oh, mighty current that can outstrip the wind
Swoop down upon our small canoe
Raise it high upon your surging crest

And cast us safely on the beach."

"And cast us safely on the beach," the others chorused.

At once a great wave lifted the boat on its crest. The canoe lept forward and rushed to the shore in a shower of foam.

The old woman tore the blanket from Kaka's back. "Hurry, hurry," she cried, jumping out of the boat and bounding toward a rocky cave.

Her husbands dashed after her, followed by Kaka. Deep into the black cavern they ran. Kaka's companions disappeared in the darkness just as the chilling "caw, caw" of a raven sounded in the distance.

The cry blotted out the soft swoosh of the waves lapping on the shore, and sent shivers down Kaka's back. He huddled in the back of the cave until he could no longer hear the raven. He searched in vain for his land otter friends.

Finally, when the rising sun painted the sand at the cave's entrance a rosy pink, Kaka crept out on the beach.

The land otter's canoe was gone, but where it had lain was a big skate. Kaka knew the land otters used skates as boats so he ran toward the large fish. It slithered into the water and swam away.

So this is the way the land otters take me home, Kaka thought – by dumping me on a lonely beach. He walked along the shore looking for a landmark that would tell him where he was. A fog bank crept in from the sea, blocking his view in all directions. If only he could see Mt. Edgecumbe. No matter how he squinted, neither through the fog or above it could he catch a glimpse of the towering peak across the water from Sitka.

At last Kaka came upon a large log swept ashore by the tide. He remembered his aunt's words. Maybe things were going according to plan after all. Kaka placed his left leg over the log and lowered himself onto it. Instantly he fell into a deep sleep.

Kaka awoke gradually. In the dreamy state between waking and sleeping he heard the whir of many flapping wings mingling with the murmur of men's voices.

"How wild he looks . . ."

"A kelp apron – why not skins?"

Kaka felt a stirring far down in his chest. A deep voice said, "It is I, my masters." Kaka knew the shaman's spirits had entered into his body and he was speaking to his own people.

When he opened his eyes he saw friends and relatives surrounding him. A great cloud of seabirds rose into the air.

"The birds led us to you," a friend explained. "We followed the beat of the shaman's drum. We found you adrift on a log with countless birds flying above you and around you."

"The birds are the spirits of the shaman," said Kaka. "They have returned me to my people."

And the power of the land otter spirits grew strong within Kaka and he became a great medicine man, foretelling events long before they happened.

It is because of Kaka's experience that many Alaskans believe in the land otter men. As recently as 1973, when two congressmen and their pilot disappeared on a flight over Alaska, the oldtimers at Klukwan whispered knowingly, "They have been captured by the land otter men."

THE END